JAY-Z

BEYONCÉ
A Biography of a Legendary Singer

ISBN 978-0-7660-4230-8

CHRIS ROCK
A Biography of a Comic Genius

ISBN 978-0-7660-4229-2

JENNIFER HUDSON
A Biography of an American Music Idol

ISBN 978-0-7660-4233-9

SEAN "DIDDY" COMBS
A Biography of a Music Mogul

ISBN 978-0-7660-4296-4

TYLER PERRY
A Biography of a Movie Mogul

ISBN 978-0-7660-4241-4

JAY-Z

A Biography of a Hip-Hop Icon

Jeff Burlingame

Enslow Publishers, Inc.
40 Industrial Road
Box 398
Berkeley Heights, NJ 07922
USA

http://www.enslow.com

Library of Congress Cataloging-in-Publication Data

Burlingame, Jeff.

Jay-Z : a biography of a hip-hop icon / Jeff Burlingame.

pages cm. — (African-American icons)

Includes index.

Summary: "Examines the life of rap artist and business entrepreneur Jay-Z, including his childhood in Brooklyn, his rise to superstardom in the music industry, his successful business ventures, his family life, and his place as the king of hip-hop"—Provided by publisher.

ISBN 978-0-7660-4232-2

1. Jay-Z, 1969—Juvenile literature. 2. Rap musicians—United States—Biography—Juvenile literature. I. Title.

ML3930.J38B87 2014

782.421649092—dc23

[B]

2013007571

Future editions:

Paperback ISBN: 978-1-4644-0407-8

EPUB ISBN: 978-1-4645-1223-0

Single-User PDF ISBN: 978-1-4646-1223-7

Multi-User PDF ISBN: 978-0-7660-5855-2

Printed in the United States of America

112013 Lake Book Manufacturing, Inc., Melrose Park, IL

10 9 8 7 6 5 4 3 2 1

To Our Readers:

We have done our best to make sure all Internet addresses in this book were active and appropriate when we went to press. However, the author and the publisher have no control over and assume no liability for the material available on those Internet sites or on other Web sites they may link to. Any comments or suggestions can be sent by e-mail to comments@enslow.com or to the address on the back cover.

♻ Enslow Publishers, Inc., is committed to printing our books on recycled paper. The paper in every book contains 10% to 30% post-consumer waste (PCW). The cover board on the outside of each book contains 100% PCW. Our goal is to do our part to help young people and the environment too!

Cover Illustration: AP Images / Matt Rourke

CONTENTS

Chapter 1

HOT AND STRONG

Legendary Madison Square Garden in New York was full of fans eager to see one last show. It had taken them less than ten minutes to snap up all twenty thousand tickets for the November 25, 2003, event, a record-setting achievement. As renowned boxing announcer Michael Buffer, dressed in all black, took to the stage to announce the performer everyone was waiting to see, the crowd's fervor hit its peak: "Ladies and gentlemen: Tonight, we come to Madison Square Garden, New York City, to see and hear a legendary superstar. From Marcy Projects, Bed-Stuy,

Brooklyn, New York. Presenting, the one, the only undisputed, undefeated heavyweight champion of the world of hip-hop. He is . . . Jayyyyyy-Z."

After Buffer ended his announcement, Jay-Z strutted onstage—wearing a black T-shirt with the face of late rapper Notorious B.I.G.—to the beat of "What More Can I Say." The song had been the first official single off his latest and rumored-to-be-final record, *The Black Album*. From the opening firework-filled moments, it was clear the concert was not going to be an average one. Everything about it was going to be special, which is just the way the rapper wanted it. It was, after all, a momentous event. This was Jay-Z's retirement show, and he planned to make it a party for the ages.

Jay-Z called upon several of his colleagues to help him out with his autobiographical set, which traced his life story from the projects he grew up in to the successful business mogul he had become. During the show, fellow stars also came out to perform, including Jay-Z's protégé, Memphis Bleek. Beanie Sigel, the Roots, Missy Elliot, Twista, Foxy Brown, Mary J. Blige, and Beyoncé were also there, as was Ghostface Killah, who popped out onstage for his moment wearing a sequined robe and several pieces of large gold jewelry.

The largest cheers of the night came when, near the end of the show, Jay-Z and singer R. Kelly hit the stage dressed in white clothing from head to toe for a few songs before Jay-Z headed offstage, leaving Kelly alone to perform three songs by himself.

When Kelly finished his third song, Jay-Z reemerged a final time, wearing a New Jersey Nets basketball jersey. He told the crowd, "I'm in heavy, heavy negotiations to bring the Nets to Brooklyn."

More than three hours into the show, Jay-Z decided he was done partying for the night, told the crowd so, and started a new song called "December 4th." The track began with a voice-over of Jay-Z's mother talking about her son's birth. Jay-Z took the song from there, rapping about how his happy childhood changed for the worse after his father left. He talked about the talent he had for rapping at a young age and the bad life decisions he made. When he was done, Jay-Z pumped his arm into the air as the stage lights followed cue of the last lyrics of the song and faded to black.

"I want to go out while I'm hot and strong," Jay-Z had said in a press release one month before his Madison Square Garden show. "The success of my recording career has opened up other opportunities for me which I want to now focus on."

Exactly what those other opportunities were remained to be seen. At the time, he was so rich that he never had to work another day in his life if he did not want to. He did not even get paid for his Madison Square Garden show. Jay-Z gave all proceeds from the concert to charity. In fact, the entire event was charity based. During the show, Jay-Z gave $25,000 checks to each of the moms of murdered rappers the Notorious B.I.G. and Tupac Shakur to use for their respective charities.

A jersey with the name of Jay-Z's record label— Roc-A-Fella—and the number 1 on it was raised to the arena's rafters at the end of the show. Then it was over. Just like that, the man who had sold millions of records, won several awards, broken several color barriers in the music world, created film and clothing companies, and made millions of dollars was done performing. Jay-Z was retiring. He was only thirty-four years old, but he felt it was time to move on. There was no more poetic way to step aside than having sold out an arena he could not afford a ticket to as a child.

Chapter 2

STREET LIFE

Jay-Z's mother may have been the only person on earth who believed her son was destined for greatness. And she believed it from the moment Shawn Corey Carter was born on December 4, 1969, in Brooklyn, New York. Gloria Carter's fourth child was a whopping ten pounds, eight ounces at birth, yet that birth was the only one that had been easy on her body. That was when, Shawn's mother said, she knew he was going to be special.

The mother's prediction was a lofty one, especially given the family's social status at the time. Shawn and his family—which included brother Eric, and sisters Michelle (Mickey) and Andrea (Annie)—were among thousands of low-income people living in the Marcy Houses, a public housing project located in the Bedford-Stuyvesant neighborhood in the New York City borough of Brooklyn.

Shawn occasionally saw extravagance on television, but there was none of it around him. Poverty was normal in the Marcy Projects, which were located in a crime-riddled area. "It wasn't safe," Shawn later told *Playboy* magazine. "Everyone there was poor and trying to get ahead. You put all those ingredients together, you have people who are willing to do anything at any time. . . . That can't be a safe environment. In each of the buildings, there's six floors, four families on each floor, three buildings connected together. Everyone's on top of everybody else. That's a powder keg [dangerous situation]."

Despite his environment, Shawn's early childhood was happy and relatively normal. He learned to ride a hand-me-down ten-speed bike when he was just four years old. His legs were not long enough for his feet to reach the pedals, so he folded them through the frame so they could. He elaborated on the bike story in an excerpt from an unreleased book he cowrote: "My uncle had promised to put training wheels on the secondhand bike I'd received from my cousin, but he hadn't gotten around to it. Me being the youngest of four kids, I was determined to be independent and not spoiled. (Although my family will tell you I am the latter.) I took the bike outside, and from 10 A.M. to 5 P.M. taught myself how to ride without training wheels. Because I was so small, my whole block in Brooklyn was watching in amazement. It was my first feeling of being famous."

The young child also banged beats on countertops. He constantly listened to Stevie Wonder, Prince, the Commodores, and Michael Jackson records in his apartment, which was the neighborhood party house. It was the place all the kids came to hang out. Jay-Z told Oprah Winfrey in 2009 that he had no clue that he was poor: "Probably the first time [I realized I was poor] was in school when I couldn't get the newest sneakers. We didn't have elaborate meals, but we didn't go without. We ate a lot of chicken. You know, 'cause chicken's cheap. We had so much chicken— chicken backs, chicken everything. To this day, I can only eat small pieces or else I feel funny."

But as the intelligent and quiet Shawn grew, his world became less fun. More real-world problems began. "For us it was great days," he told TV talk show host David Letterman years later. "It was fun, and ice cream man . . . but then some days it would turn super violent. You had these extreme highs and lows."

Often, drugs fueled that violence. Occasionally, Shawn's family would get wrapped up in it. When he was nine years old, Shawn witnessed a neighbor boy dropped to the ground by a bullet. The same year, his Uncle Ray was murdered. Shawn's father set out on a long-term, alcohol-fueled quest to find his brother's killer. "The tragedy—compounded by the injustice—drove him crazy, sent him to the bottle, and ultimately became a factor in the unraveling of my parents' marriage," he wrote later in a book he released called *Decoded*.

That marriage unraveled completely in 1980, when Shawn was eleven years old. That is when his father left the house and never returned. Gloria Carter's office clerk job became the sole source of income for the family. She was able to fill the financial void but not the paternal one left in a child who would not see his father again for more than twenty years. Shawn told Winfrey in 2009 how he felt about his father leaving:

> Anger. At the whole situation. Because when you're growing up, your dad is your superhero. Once you've let yourself fall that in love with someone, once you put him on such a high pedestal and he lets you down, you never want to experience that pain again. So I remember just being really quiet and really cold.

Never wanting to let myself get close to someone like that again. I carried that feeling throughout my life, until my father and I met up before he died.

His father's absence did allow him to grow much closer to his only remaining parent. On more than one occasion, Shawn has called his mother his best friend.

Still, the smart, quiet kid grew quieter after his father left. Years later, Shawn's sixth-grade teacher, Renee Rosenblum-Lowden, talked about her famous student. "I knew he was very bright," she said in a press release for her 2008 book, *You Have to Go to School . . . You're the Teacher!* "But what I remember very specifically is that he never smiled. He had a lot of problems in his life, like all my students did. But when I would make a joke and he smiled, it would literally light up the room."

Jay-Z gave his former teacher credit for helping him succeed. He told *Forbes* magazine in 2008: "There was this one sixth-grade teacher named Miss Lowden. She must have seen something in me, and she gave me this attention and this love for words. . . . She took us on a field trip to her house, which opened me up to the world. . . . My imagination grew from there."

Shawn also became more independent after his father left. He told Winfrey he "felt protective of my mom. I remember telling her, 'Don't worry, when I get big, I'm going to take care of this.' I felt like I had to step up. I was eleven years old, right? But I felt I had to make the situation better."

As many children raised without fathers do, particularly those living in impoverished places such as the Marcy Projects, Shawn began spending more time on the streets and getting into trouble. When he was twelve years old, that trouble included shooting his drug-addicted brother in the shoulder for stealing jewelry and other items from the family. "I never used crack, [but] I'd seen my brother. After my father, that was the next person I looked up to," Jay-Z said during a 2003 interview. "He had all the girls, he played basketball. Then he was a whole different person [once he started using]. . . . My brother was a really, really, really tough person to get along with. He was messed up on drugs really bad."

The drugs that his brother was involved with soon took over Shawn's life too. Shawn became a street hustler at age thirteen, doing anything he could to make money and buy the fancy cars he saw young black men from the projects show up in sometimes. That included selling drugs of all types, such as marijuana, heroin, and crack. A newly popular drug, crack was made by mixing the expensive drug cocaine with baking soda and other ingredients to form a crystallized product that could be cut into "rocks" and sold cheaply.

Crack's cheapness, and its addictiveness, made it the drug of choice for those in Shawn's neighborhood and eventually in inner cities across the United States. "[Crack] was a plague in that neighborhood. It was just everywhere, everywhere you look. In the hallways. You could smell it in the hallways," he told *CBS News* in 2008. "Back then, it was like, I would say it was, like, two things. It was either you're doin' it or you was movin' it."

Shawn Carter was movin' it—quickly. He got wrapped up in the drug culture, which included guns. One time, a boy he considered a friend fired three shots at him from close range with a machine gun, somehow missing all three times. He has never publicly explained why his friend shot at him.

He knew the potential damage the drug world had in store for him. Yet, he chose to continue. "I wasn't blind to the damage that I was causing myself and other people when I was in the game," he wrote in his book *Decoded*. "I wasn't deluded about the fact that my motivations went beyond satisfying my basic material needs—that I also loved the excitement and the status of that life." Basically, he was making a lot of money dealing drugs, buying things he never dreamed he would be able to afford.

His crack providers grew to love Shawn too, because he could sell their product fast and did not use it himself. His days as a crack dealer were both kind and unkind. As he recalled later: "I lost people I loved, was betrayed by people I trusted, felt the breeze of bullets flying by my head. I saw crack addiction destroy families—it almost destroyed mine—but I sold it, too. . . . I went dead broke and got hood rich on those streets. I hated it."

There were positive activities going on in Shawn's neighborhood as well. Sometimes he and other kids would play basketball and baseball at nearby parks. Sometimes they would form circles around boys who were rapping lyrics—freestyle or rehearsed—to try to get a rise from the crowd.

One Marcy rapper named Slate left a lasting impression on young Shawn. Most of the time, Slate was an average kid. But "In the circle," Shawn later wrote, "he was transformed, like the church ladies touched by the spirit, and everyone was mesmerized. He was rhyming, throwing out couplet after couplet like he was in a trance, for a crazy long time—thirty minutes straight off the top of his head, never losing the beat, riding the handclaps. He rhymed about nothing. . . . He never stopped moving, not dancing, just rotating in the center of the circle, looking for his next target."

Witnessing Slate's actions—and the crowd's positive reaction—hooked young Shawn like no drug ever could or would. "I *could* do *that*," he thought. At that moment, his life changed forever.

He began writing poetry in what he called his "notebook," which actually was sheets of paper held together by a paper clip. He had other "real" notebooks too. One of them he hid under his bed every night so no one would steal it. Soon, he did not need to write anything down. He memorized his words. He told *Rolling Stone* magazine, "I had this green notebook with no lines in it, and I used to write all crooked. I wrote every damn day. Then I started running around in the streets, and that's how not writing came about. I was comin' up with these ideas, and I'd write 'em on a paper bag, and I had all these paper bags in my pocket, and I hate a lot of things in my pocket, so I started memorizing. . . ."

He practiced rapping constantly. His lyrics oftentimes were filled with rage created by his father's departure, the chaotic drug world around him, and his impoverished life in the projects. Soon, he *was* Slate, the one with the circle formed around him, its members watching his every move, hanging on his every word. The words came from his notebooks. They came from his memory. Sometimes, he just made them up on the fly. His rapping earned him the nickname Jazzy. That eventually was shortened to the stage name the world would one day know him by: Jay-Z.

When Jay-Z was coming of age, rap music—also known as hip-hop, which technically is the culture the music form stems from—still was a relatively new form of music. Rap is defined as rhyming to a musical beat. Its origins have been traced back to early African oral history. However, most historians agree that its modern-day birth occurred during the 1970s in New York City's South Bronx, a poor borough similar to the Brooklyn neighborhood Jay-Z was from.

Credit for bringing rap to a mainstream audience in the United States frequently is given to a group from New Jersey called the Sugarhill Gang. In 1979, the Sugarhill Gang had a Top-40 hit with a lengthy song called "Rapper's Delight." In the song, the group's three young members took turns rapping over the top of a beat from a song called "Good Times" by a band named Chic. Using another group's song was called sampling. It was a technique that became common in the rap industry.

The popularity of "Rapper's Delight" not only landed the Sugarhill Gang on the radio, but it also earned the group a spot on some national television shows. One of those was called *Soul Train*. *Soul Train* was highly influential to African Americans across the United States. The musical variety show featured dancing and music. It was one of the few programs on national television that featured African-American culture. An African American named Don Cornelius hosted it.

Jay-Z was one of *Soul Train's* many viewers. He and his family—and many others in Marcy Projects—gathered around the television to watch it every Saturday afternoon. Jay-Z later wrote in his memoir *Decoded,* " [W]hen my big sister Annie and I saw Don Cornelius introduce the Sugar Hill [sic] Gang, we just stopped in the middle of the living room with our jaws open. What are *they* doing on TV?"

The Carter children could not believe their eyes. On their television were three black men that looked like they could have been their neighbors. It was not something you would see on TV every day. Jay-Z found it inspirational. "Our little world was all we knew. We didn't know anything outside of that world," he told CNN. "So to look and see people that look like you achieving great things . . . it improves self-esteem. It improves upon self-worth. A lot of choices are made from the position of 'my life is not worth much. This sort of living is not much, so if I risk my life, what am I really missing?' But if you know how valuable human life is you have more respect for yours and for others."

The success of the Sugarhill Gang opened the door for other black hip-hop artists, including New Yorkers Run-DMC and Kool Moe Dee. Many of those artists directly and deeply influenced the aspiring rapper Jay-Z. He realized at that point that pushing drugs was not the only way to make it out of the projects. There was another way out, another way to obtain a flashy car, fancy clothes, jewelry, and money. Another way to escape.

Jay-Z was convinced he could do what the Sugarhill Gang and others that followed them had done. And that is what he set out to do. "[Music] was a way out of my environment," Jay-Z told *MySpace* in 2009. "I was into a lot of crazy things. I saw this as my escape and my way out. I wanted to take that and transform that into a career for myself in business. I didn't have any aspirations to be a superstar, I just wanted to have a job."

He never knew rapping his poetry could be a job. Until he saw the Sugarhill Gang.

After that point, Jay-Z's lyric-filled notebooks followed him everywhere. That even included into the classrooms of his high school in Brooklyn. Jay-Z went to the same school as Trevor Smith, Jr., later known as Busta Rhymes, and Christopher Wallace, later known as both Biggie Smalls and the Notorious B.I.G. Both those boys would eventually become rap stars in their own right. In high school, though, they were simply wannabes.

Occasionally, the three aspiring rappers would battle each other lyrically. Busta Rhymes told MTV he remembered battling Jay-Z one time in the high school cafeteria:

> At the time, when we were rhyming, it was speed rap. That was the thing to do. I knew how to freak it, and he knew how to freak it. And at the time, he was so ill. He kind of got the best of the situation. I got to give it up. He was so ill and his arsenal was so long that he had more than what I did. I spit my one rap, and my tank was empty real fast. He came with two or three after that, and I was like, "Here we go." But I gave it my best. . . . That was probably the first time that I lost a battle that mattered. [Jay-Z] always exemplified greatness as an MC. He was a scientist with it.

Jay-Z later talked about his interactions with Biggie Smalls and Busta Rhymes too. "Big, he would never talk about rap or anything like that. He was just there. And Busta was always talkin' about rapping." Jay-Z also recalled to *MySpace* his version of the lunchtime battle with Busta Rhymes: "I got him good. I was rappin' pretty fast and no one was expecting that type of, that level of, acrobatics. I used to catch people off guard with that. . . . When I brought out the fast stuff, it was over."

By the time he was in high school, Jay-Z had hooked up with a similarly fast-mouthed rapper from the neighborhood named Jonathan "Jaz-O" Burks. Jaz-O, also known as Jaz and Big Jaz, had minor musical successes as a performer and as a producer. Jay-Z looked up to Jaz-O. The older man served as a mentor to the younger Jay-Z.

In the late 1980s, when Jaz-O landed a record deal, that connection paid off. Jaz-O brought the nineteen-year-old Jay-Z with him to live in London for a month. That was where the record label had sent him to record his album. The two young men shared an apartment there. Jay-Z, who had dropped out of high school a little more than a year earlier, later wrote, ". . . everything about the trip to London—going to Rockefeller Center to get my passport, packing for a month-long trip, preparing for a trans-Atlantic flight— was new for me. It was a surreal, disorienting experience: two [guys] from Marcy in a flat in Notting Hill."

Before Jay-Z left Brooklyn, he worked hard to make sure his drug-selling business was in good shape. He made sure his clients were all taken care of. He wanted to be certain the business would be there for him when he returned. He told Winfrey, "I was preparing to come back to the streets because I always had a fear that this music thing wouldn't be successful."

Jaz-O let Jay-Z rap on some songs on the album he recorded in London, which was called *Word to the Jaz*. He also let Jay-Z perform on some songs on his next album, *To Your Soul*. The songs included "Hawaiian Sophie" and "The Originators." The first one was a humorous, ukulele-filled tale about, of course, a Hawaiian girl named Sophie that Jaz-O wanted to date. Jay-Z only spoke a few words on the song, which sounded like a rip-off of the style of Will Smith, a successful rapper from Philadelphia, Pennsylvania, who recorded under the name the Fresh Prince. The label's goal was to turn Jaz-O into a newer Fresh Prince. It did not work.

Jay-Z had a far more significant role on "The Originators." He costarred with Jaz-O both in the song's video and during the performance of the song on the popular American TV program *Yo! MTV Raps*. The program was influential and important to the world of hip-hop music because it allowed millions of viewers the opportunity to see the genre's stars on a regular basis.

Jay-Z only briefly appeared on Jaz-O's third album. It was released in 1991, two years after his first one had been. By that time, it was obvious Jaz-O was not going to be the next Fresh Prince and his chances at success were all but over. But Jay-Z continued to make guest appearances on other rappers' songs, including a few produced by a hip-hop group called Original Flavor. Jay-Z's work with Original Flavor included rapping a lengthy verse on one of the group's singles, "Can I Get Open."

Everyone who listened to the song found it obvious that Jay-Z's skills as an MC were far superior to those of the Original Flavor members he shared time rapping with on the song. It may have been Original Flavor's record, but Jay-Z was the star. During this time, Jay-Z also had a starring role as a fast-paced rapper on the song "Show and Prove," which became a minor hit for fellow Brooklyn rapper Antonio "Big Daddy Kane" Hardy.

Jay-Z was nearly twenty-five years old when "Show and Prove" was released. He later said that was the point in life where he was at a crossroads. He faced a big decision. He had never had what most people would consider a "real" job. None of the ways he had ever made money to date seemed appealing in the long run. Selling drugs, which by now he was doing in several states and making large amounts of money, had lost its appeal. "I started seeing people go to jail and get killed, and the light slowly came on. I was like, 'This life has no good ending,'" he told Winfrey.

But rapping on other artists' records—and being in the music industry in general—did not seem like the greatest career choice either. Even though he himself was a law-breaking hustler, Jay-Z did not feel record executives had much integrity. He felt they did not care about the rappers or their albums they were releasing. To Jay-Z, record labels were only out to make themselves rich. He told Winfrey, "[When] Jaz's album didn't work out . . . the same record label tried to sign me, but Jaz was the one who'd brought me in, and I felt that signing wouldn't be loyal to him. So I told them no. I didn't want to be involved with those record guys. They weren't stand-up people."

Winfrey found Jay-Z's stance ironic. She said, "[Y]ou, a drug dealer, couldn't trust the guys in the record business, as if they had no integrity."

"Exactly," Jay-Z told her. "[Integrity is] doing the right thing. . . . In the streets there's a certain respect level. If two drug dealers make it to a certain level, they show a certain respect when they see each other. It's bad business for them to be warring."

Still, Jay-Z continued to pursue a career in music. He was far more into it than he was into dealing drugs. Rapping was where his passion was. Rapping was where his talent was. Jay-Z's goal was to be a solo rapper. He wanted his name, not someone else's, to be on the record covers. He wanted his name to be announced when a song was played on the radio. He wanted to have his own record deal.

He said to Winfrey, "I'd been trying to transition from the streets to the music business, but I would make demos and then quit for six months. And I started to realize that I couldn't be successful until I let the street life go. My mom always taught me—you know, little boys listen to their moms too much—that whatever you put into something is what you're going to get out of it. I had to fully let go of what I was doing before for the music to be successful. That was a leap of faith for me. I said, 'I have to give this everything.'"

He began doing just that. Jay-Z gave up his life of dealing drugs and began to focus only on music. His life—and the music industry in general—would soon be forever changed because of it.

Chapter 3

BREAKING BIG

To achieve the type of success Jay-Z was looking for—to become a successful solo hip-hop artist—he had to return to the same place he had needed to escape from to give his ambition a shot. That place was the streets. Jay-Z made a demo CD and tried to market it to record labels. He did not have any success. He sold copies of the song "I Can't Go For That" out of the back of his car. Nothing worked until he recorded a single called "In My Lifetime" with the help of Ski, a member of Original Flavor.

The hard work finally paid off. "In My Lifetime" was an underground hit. So much so, that a small label called Payday Records decided to sign Jay-Z to a deal. He now had what he was looking for—a record contract. Jay-Z was happy. But he soon found out that having a deal was not as great as he once believed it would be. His deal was only worth $25,000, and the label did not treat him well.

He told *Yahoo! Music* in 1999:

> [Payday Records was] acting shady the whole time, like they didn't know how to work a record or something. . . . The things that they were setting up for me I could have done myself. They had me traveling places to do instores [short performances in record stores], and my product wasn't even available in the store. We shot one video, but when the time came for me to do the video for the second single, I had to be cut out. They gave me the money and I started my own company. There was a little arguing back and forth, but our conflict finally got resolved. The bottom line was they wasn't doing their job, so I had to get out of there.

Jay-Z took the money and, with the help of a couple of others, decided to produce an entire album on his own. One of the men who helped Jay-Z was Damon "Dame" Dash, a music manager from Brooklyn. Jay-Z had been introduced to Dash by Clark Kent, a popular DJ who worked with many hip-hop artists at the time. Dash also signed on to be Jay-Z's manager. He and Jay-Z, along with Kareem "Biggs" Burke, started a record label in the process. They called it Roc-A-Fella Records.

Roc-A-Fella had one basic goal: to release Jay-Z's records on its own, without the help of a major label. The reason was simple too. Major labels take huge cuts of what the artists they sign make. The artist—the person who created the music—usually gets a small percentage of his or her record sales. Jay-Z and the rest of his team did not believe that was fair. They wanted to keep all the money from records they sold. To do so, they would need to start their own record label.

Roc-A-Fella Records was named after John D. Rockefeller, an oil tycoon from New York who lived from 1839 to 1937 and once was the richest man in the United States. The name signified the label's goals for success. Those goals were grand. Especially because the trio chose the name before they had accomplished anything. In time, the name choice proved to be an appropriate one.

In 1996, Roc-A-Fella released Jay-Z's first record. It was called *Reasonable Doubt*. The record's cover featured a photo of a cigar-smoking Jay-Z, his head pointed down and his face half-covered by a black hat. Recorded in a New York studio and released in June, *Reasonable Doubt* was full of autobiographical tales of Jay-Z's life to that point. On the record, he rapped about his troubled childhood and hustling. Those true stories gave *Reasonable Doubt* a personal depth many critics believe helped make it the classic it eventually became.

Of course, there was plenty of rap's stereotypical superfluity as well, including the opening track, "Can't Knock the Hustle." That song took listeners on a slow-paced trek through a day in the life of a "successful" street dealer: fine cars, money, and women. *Reasonable Doubt's* other singles included "Dead Presidents II" and "Feelin' It." The album's songs included some noteworthy, or soon to be, guest performers, including Mary J. Blige, the Notorious B.I.G., and Foxy Brown. *Reasonable Doubt* was twenty-six years of Jay-Z's life, all wrapped up in an hour-long package. Unless he waited until he was in his mid-fifties, Jay-Z would never have that much of his life to talk about again.

Reasonable Doubt's singles all cracked the Billboard Hot 100 chart when they were released. The album itself eventually made it all the way to number 23 in the United States. *Reasonable Doubt* showcased Jay-Z's vocal dexterity and his ability to rap in different styles and at different speeds.

The album helped grow louder the buzz that had been surrounding Jay-Z and the Roc-A-Fella label. Critics—who can make or break an album by writing good or bad things about it—loved *Reasonable Doubt*. About the album, *Allmusic* said, "A hungry young MC with a substantial underground buzz drops an instant classic of a debut, detailing his experiences on the streets with disarming honesty, and writing some of the most acrobatic rhymes heard in quite some time" and that the record was "one of the finest albums of New York's hip-hop renaissance of the '90s."

As time wore on, Jay-Z looked back fondly on *Reasonable Doubt* as his favorite album. He told Oprah Winfrey in 2009 that was because it contained so much of his life. "All the emotions and experiences of 26 years came out in it," he said. With the childhood and young adult life he had lived, Jay-Z had a lot to write about.

Fans loved the record too. They bought nearly a half-million copies of *Reasonable Doubt* in the first six months it was on the market. Such sales were modest compared to what he one day would garner. But they were enough for Jay-Z and friends to continue to grow the Roc-A-Fella brand.

They promoted their brand and *Reasonable Doubt* several different ways, according to one of the album's producers, David "Ski Beatz" Willis. "It was everything, word of mouth, battling, live shows, everything," he told *Soul Culture* magazine in 2011. "Jay would battle anybody on site, go to different places and just battle. He battled DMX, had a battle with Big L, he had a battle with LL Cool J. He did a lot of local shows and every time he did the show, the buzz was getting bigger and bigger because he was the best lyricist that anyone had heard and his stage presence was crazy; everything about him just transcended on stage. The word got out that Jay-Z was coming . . . "

Jay-Z and his partners rented an office for Roc-A-Fella in a poor section of downtown New York, an area *Yahoo! Music* described as " . . . one of the dreariest parts of the busiest city in the world. Storefronts housing $10 clothing stores, watch repair shops and hot dog huts line the narrow, dark, seemingly haunted streets."

Although Jay-Z was rapping about living the high life, he certainly was not there yet. This was fine by him. *Yahoo! Music* reported that Jay-Z said:

I don't mind being down here in this area, because this is just a starting point for us. I like being away from everybody right now, because I can get all my stuff together, then I can move uptown with all those other [people] when everything's straight. No sense in spending a whole lot of money on office space and moving employees round if your product isn't bringing in any money yet—that's a mistake executives make. I used my money to get this label off the ground and that was the right decision.

Jay-Z thought his next "right decision" would be to sign his old friend Jaz-O to the label. He wanted to help produce records for the mentor who had helped him get his start in the business. For various reasons, Jaz-O decided not to join his protégé at Roc-A-Fella. This created a feud between the two former friends that would last a long time and play out on several recordings each would make.

In 1997, Jay-Z signed a distribution deal with a large company called Def Jam. Distribution deals are how record labels get their music to stores, where the public can buy it. No matter how good the record (especially at the time when the Internet was not a reliable way to download music), without a distribution deal, no one would hear it. Or be able to buy it. Roc-A-Fella's large deal now meant the next album Jay-Z produced would be available in many more locations than the first one, which had only been available in some stores and cities.

All the pieces were now in place for Jay-Z's second album to succeed. First, he needed to write and record it. As Jay-Z was writing music and lining up performers to join him on his much-anticipated second record, tragedy struck.

Shortly after midnight on March 9, his high school friend and current collaborator, Christopher Wallace, aka the Notorious B.I.G. and Biggie Smalls, was murdered as he was leaving a party in Los Angeles following the Soul Train Music Awards show. The Soul Train Music Awards were created by the same people responsible for the *Soul Train* TV show Jay-Z watched as a child.

Many believed Wallace was killed in retaliation for the recent death of his rival rapper, Tupac Shakur. Shakur had been murdered six months earlier during a drive-by shooting in Las Vegas, Nevada. He worked for a label called Death Row Records and had been the star of the West Coast rappers. For years, rappers on the West Coast had been feuding lyrically—and sometimes physically—with Wallace and other rappers on the East Coast. Some people believed that Wallace had been involved with Shakur's murder, but there has never been any clear evidence that this was the case.

Whatever the reason for his murder, twenty-four-year-old Wallace was dead. Jay-Z, now twenty-seven, was devastated. He had spoken with his friend just an hour before he was murdered. The death had an impact on the making of Jay-Z's next album. "I don't have him to bounce [ideas] off of," Jay-Z told MTV at the time of Wallace's death. "You have to find different other ways to really motivate yourself. We're all sad for selfish reasons. I know I'm sad I don't get to talk to him every day. He can't make me laugh. I can't go to the studio and hear what he's working on."

In another tribute, Jay-Z told *Billboard* magazine, "His passing was tragic to me, because he's one of those rare guys. I mean, I don't really vibe with everybody, but he and I clicked so well. We lived, like, fifteen minutes away from each other, and we thought alike, because we come from the same place."

For a short time following the murder, police in Los Angeles would not allow Jay-Z to perform in California because of death threats he and other East Coast rappers received. "That whole coastal war was something that happened on wax [records] and got outta hand simply because of the power of the two people involved," Jay-Z told *Blues & Soul* in 1998. "People were willing to do ANYTHING for them, even when they didn't fully understand the situation."

Jay-Z has repeatedly said in interviews he does not believe rap music had anything to do with the murders of either Tupac or Biggie. For the most part, Jay-Z steered clear of the East Coast–West Coast rap battle.

He was a lot safer for having done so. If anything good came out of the deaths of Tupac and the Notorious B.I.G., it was that the coastal rap war died down soon after. Hip-hop music, for the most part, started moving in a more positive direction.

The Notorious B.I.G.'s second studio album, the eerily titled *Life After Death*, was released just two weeks after Biggie was murdered. Jay-Z made an appearance on the album's seventh track, "I Love the Dough." *Life After Death* quickly became the number one record in the country. Three of its songs were nominated for Grammy Awards. The record's success helped elevate Jay-Z's status as well. It was a strange coincidence. The death of one Brooklyn artist led the public to appreciate and anticipate the next release of another prominent Brooklyn artist even more.

They received that surviving artist's release later that year, 1997, when Jay-Z's second record was released. *In My Lifetime, Vol. 1* was in many ways different from *Reasonable Doubt*. Going into the recording of the album, Jay-Z had told *Billboard* magazine: "I want people to compare the two albums to a relationship with a girl. Most times when you meet her, it's physical. And the first album dealt with things on the outside—the cars, the jewelry, the clothes . . . things you could see. Now that everyone got to know that, I'm gonna take 'em a little deeper."

The most obvious difference in the two albums was evident upon first listen. It had nothing to do with the depth of the lyrics. Rather, it was the production of the songs. Each one on the second album was far more polished and less raw, thanks in part to the album's producers. They came from the record label Bad Boy Records of superstar rapper Sean "Puff Daddy" Combs, who was a friend of Biggie Smalls and had produced music with him. Secondly, the song's structures were different than they had been on Jay-Z's first record. *In My Lifetime, Vol. 1* was filled with catchier, less-sophisticated—but no less gritty— lyrics. Those wondering if Jay-Z was going to face what in the music and entertainment industry is called a "sophomore slump," received their answers once music critics reviewed the record.

Allmusic gave it a near-perfect four-and-a-half-star rating, saying Jay-Z created "some of the best rapping heard in the rap game since the deaths of 2Pac and The Notorious B.I.G." *Vibe* magazine was a little more lukewarm. It said Jay-Z's new record " . . . will surely enjoy a healthy dose of mainstream consumption. But both playas and haters can be assured that Jay-Z's new, easy-to-swallow coating dulls the ruff 'n' ready active ingredient that made his first release the classic cure."

In My Lifetime, Vol. 1's list of guest stars was longer than it had been on *Reasonable Doubt*. Foxy Brown returned this time, performing alongside Jay-Z and Babyface on the record's second single, "(Always Be My) Sunshine." But there were new performers too, including Lil' Kim and Puff Daddy ("I Know What Girls Like"), and Blackstreet ("The City Is Mine"). *In My Lifetime, Vol. 1* also included "Who Ya Wit II," a slightly different version of a song that had been released on the soundtrack to the movie *Sprung* earlier that year.

"Streets Is Watching," which Jay-Z said is the last song of his that Biggie Smalls ever heard, was also on *In My Lifetime*. Jay-Z said the late rapper had enjoyed the tune. So much, in fact, that he asked Jay-Z to play it for him so many times that he eventually gave him a copy of the song for himself before it was released.

Jay-Z's hard-core fans were hesitant to accept his slick new songs. But by the same token, that slickness—which sometimes made the songs sound as if they could be classified as pop instead of rap—and the help of heavy marketing and promotion from both Roc-A-Fella and Def Jam, helped Jay-Z reach a much larger audience than he had the first time around. Jay-Z was well aware of what he was doing.

With some harder-edged songs sprinkled in to appease those who liked that side of his work, *In My Lifetime, Vol. 1* debuted as the number three record in the country. Each of its three singles found its way into the top one hundred. It sold more than one million copies, but Jay-Z was not completely satisfied with the record. He told *AOL Music*, "[*Reasonable Doubt*] was a cult classic on the streets, but it wasn't successful in the music business and [with *In My Lifetime, Vol. 1*] I tried to blend the two. If you look back on *In My Lifetime*, there were songs on there that were brilliant. [But] I don't listen to that album because I think I messed it up. I think I missed having two classics in a row [by] trying to get on the radio. . . . I don't have any regrets but musically, the album [is] the one that got away." Despite his later-day regrets, Jay-Z did accomplish his goal at the time. *In My Lifetime* was constantly played on the radio.

Exactly how quickly Jay-Z realized the album had gotten away from him is unknown. Many biographical histories of Jay-Z's long career simply gloss over *In My Lifetime, Vol. 1* and skip straight from Jay-Z's first to his third album. That album was called *Vol. 2 . . . Hard Knock Life*. It was released less than a year after *In My Lifetime*.

Critics believed *Hard Knock Life* would be the record to catapult Jay-Z from the underground to the mainstream. With the help of the title song "Hard Knock Life (Ghetto Anthem)"—and guest stars Foxy Brown, DMX, West Coast rapper Too $hort, Memphis Bleek, Ja Rule, and others—that is what happened.

Jay-Z's third album debuted at number one in the United States on the Billboard charts.

There was a good reason for the record's success. *Hard Knock Life* was the perfect combination of the two styles and approaches Jay-Z had taken with his first two albums. *Vol. 2 . . . Hard Knock Life* was as radio-friendly as *In My Lifetime* had been, which helped it appeal to those who normally would not listen to rap music. At the same time, *Hard Knock Life* contained rough-and-tumble lyrics, just as *Reasonable Doubt* had.

For example, the song "Hard Knock Life (Ghetto Anthem)" sampled the innocence of the song of the same name from the Broadway musical *Annie* and combined it with Jay-Z's "hard-knock" story of hustling on the streets, drugs, and gun violence. Most reviewers loved the balance Jay-Z finally had reached. He had found the perfect combination of grit and glitz.

"His next move seemed like a certain coffin-nailer," *Rolling Stone* wrote about Jay-Z's release of both *Hard Knock Life* and the "Hard Knock Life (Ghetto Anthem)" single. "He sampled the theme song from the musical *Annie* and turned it into an inescapable summer pop-rap crossover hit . . . [which] took him from the ears of the [experts] to the disc-changers of casual rap fans."

In his book *Decoded*, Jay-Z said, "I felt the chorus to that song perfectly captured what little kids in the ghetto felt every day: "Stead of kisses, we get kicked.' We might not all have literally been orphans, but a whole generation of us had basically raised ourselves in the streets."

Jay-Z told *Blues & Soul* his use of the *Annie* song was a reflection of his eclectic musical taste. As a child, he explained, he had listened to all kinds of music. "The average kid growing up in the ghetto is forced to listen to only R&B 'cause that's his parents' taste and the only thing they play all the time. With me, because my moms and pops had such a big record collection with the widest range of music, as I grew older I started experimenting and listening to different styles. So these days I believe there's only two types of music—good and bad."

While the catchiness of "Hard Knock Life (Ghetto Anthem)" was difficult to overlook, so too was the rawness and anger in many of the album's thirteen other tracks. In "Nigga What, Nigga Who (Originator 99)" to "Money, Cash, Hoes" and "Can I Get A . . . ," Jay-Z did not shy away from talking about the street life he once led or the life of luxury he was now beginning to live. He told *Blues & Soul*: "With this album I was really in a zone—I've never been so comfortable and content recording. I was like

(Michael) Jordan that night when he hit nine threes and he walked off the court like 'I'm HOT! I can't MISS right now!' . . . I honestly think I was in the best recording mode of my life. And creatively, I felt like I put everyone in the right place. With my guests, I felt like a conductor directing a concerto."

Though his music was the main reason for the luxurious life he was now living, it was not the only reason. Jay-Z and Roc-A-Fella had expanded their business too. They began producing records of other musicians, created a clothing line, and even dabbled in making movies. "I see myself as so much more than a rapper," Jay-Z told *Blues & Soul* at the time.

In 1999, Jay-Z and Damon Dash created Rocawear, a brand of clothing geared toward urban youth. Dash handled the business end of the company, while Jay-Z's main role was to provide creative input on product development and also to wear the clothing onstage and in appearances to help promote it.

On the music front, Jay-Z's Hard Knock Life tour sold out arenas across the United States. The two-month-long tour visited fifty-four cities and also included Method Man, Redman, and co-headliner DMX. The *San Francisco Chronicle* reviewed an April show in nearby San Jose: "Bounding across the stage in black athletic gear, Jay-Z appeared relaxed and in casual control. Occasionally, glancing around the arena, he offered a covert smile, as if he liked what he saw but wasn't about to give anyone the satisfaction of knowing it."

When the Hard Knock Life tour stopped in Denver, Colorado, on April 27, Jay-Z and DMX donated the money they made that night to help the families of the victims from the deadly massacre at nearby Columbine High School one week earlier. "We decided to donate the proceeds from this show as soon as we saw the date on the schedule," Jay-Z told MTV. "It was never a question. . . . We've known firsthand how pointless and senseless violence always is, and we wanted to show our support in a real way."

By the end of the tour, Jay-Z had established himself as one of the top rap performers in the country. He also saw himself as a spokesperson for others. "I really believe I'm the voice for a lot of people who don't have that microphone or who can't rap," Jay-Z told *Blues & Soul*.

Being the voice for others had its downside. With his increasing popularity came an increase in critics. Jay-Z often found himself as the whipping boy for people and organizations that felt his misogynistic, swearing- and hate-term-filled lyrics set a bad example for America's youth. Such youth included those who were growing up in the same ghettos in New York and elsewhere Jay-Z had hoped to positively influence. The same ghettos he himself had grown up in.

During a 2009 interview, Oprah Winfrey asked Jay-Z about his frequent use of the word *nigger* and *nigga,* both of which are derogatory, racist, and hurtful terms for African Americans. Those words often are censored and called the "N-word." Winfrey, who is also black, did not like Jay-Z using the term. The word is derived from the word *negro,* which means "black." During the seventeenth through the nineteenth centuries, white slave owners in the United States called their black slaves "niggers" as a means of degradation.

"Do you believe that using the N-word is necessary?" Oprah asked Jay-Z. "When I hear the N-word, I still think about every black man who was lynched—and the N-word was the last thing he heard."

"Nothing is necessary," Jay-Z responded. "It's just become part of the way we communicate. My generation hasn't had the same experience with that word that generations of people before us had. We weren't so close to the pain. So in our way, we disarmed the word. We took the fire pin out of the grenade. . . . I believe that a speaker's intention is what gives a word its power. And if we eliminate the N-word, other words would just take its place."

Vol. 2 . . . Hard Knock Life won a Grammy Award for Best Rap Album in 1999. The Grammys are considered the highest award someone in the music business can obtain. But Jay-Z refused to attend the prestigious ceremony to receive his award because he did not feel the award committee gave enough respect to hip-hop music. Also, his friend DMX had not been nominated for the great record Jay-Z felt he had recorded.

In late 1999, Jay-Z and a host of other well-known producers and musicians made another record fans and music critics could not get enough of. Called *Vol. 3 . . . Life and Times of S. Carter,* Jay-Z's latest record picked up where he had left off. It combined his frequently fast-paced flow with several celebrity guest vocalists and producers into a fifteen-song package that again debuted atop the Billboard charts. The album's singles included "Do It Again (Put Ya Hands Up)," "Big Pimpin'," and "Things That U Do," which featured superstar Mariah Carey on vocals.

Vol. 3 . . . Life and Times of S. Carter sold nearly a half-million copies in the first week it was available for purchase. That sales number would have been far higher had an early leaked copy of the CD not found its way to the streets a month before its official release date. That event sent Jay-Z into a tailspin. He could not stand to see his record hit the streets before it was supposed to. It cost him and others a lot of money, particularly because, with the popularity of the Internet, the music was made available across the world for free.

"I was totally at a loss," he wrote in *Decoded*. "This was really too much. I was flipping out on Def Jam [his record label] staff, accusing people of having something to do with the bootleg copies on the street. I just couldn't believe how flagrant it was, and how much more damaging it could be than the usual low-level bootlegging."

Then Jay-Z began trying to figure out who had leaked the record. People who thought they knew kept giving him the name of the same person. On December 2, 1999, at a record-release party in Manhattan for rapper Q-Tip, Jay-Z ran into the man many people accused of being behind the bootleg. Jay-Z decided to confront the man about it. He did, then went back to his table. Then, Jay-Z wrote in *Decoded*, "Before I even realized what I was doing, I headed back over to him, but this time I was blacking out with anger. The next thing I knew, all hell had broken loose in the club."

That "hell" included Jay-Z stabbing producer Lance "Un" Rivera at least twice with a five-inch knife. Rivera was hospitalized, treated for his wounds, and released. Jay-Z left the club and went into hiding for a few days after the incident but eventually turned himself in to police for questioning. He did not admit he had done anything. In fact, Jay-Z proclaimed his innocence for nearly two years. Some even believed the stabbing was staged by Jay-Z to draw publicity for his new album. Jay-Z has denied that.

The stabbing case was scheduled to go to trial. Eventually, Jay-Z pleaded guilty a few days before his 2001 trial date, after he and his bodyguard were arrested when police found a gun on the bodyguard. Jay-Z could have been sent to prison for fifteen years if a trial had been held and a jury had found him guilty. That was the maximum sentence for the crime he committed—felony assault in the second degree. Instead, Jay-Z was sentenced to three years' probation because he admitted his guilt. Jay-Z believed that moment was a life changer.

"I realized that I had a choice in life," Jay-Z later wrote. "There was no reason to put my life on the line, and the lives of everyone who depends on me, because of a momentary loss of control. . . . I vowed to never allow myself to be in a situation like that again."

Chapter 4

FADE TO BLACK

I f the late-1999 stabbing incident affected Jay-Z at all, it did not appear to have an impact on the amazing rate at which he and Roc-A-Fella were able to produce quality recordings.

The large amount of time Jay-Z spent in recording studios was well known. So was the unique way in which he went about recording his songs. Jay-Z never wrote down any lyrics. He just memorized them. Producer Gimel "Young Guru" Keaton spoke to *Sound on Sound* magazine in 2009 about Jay-Z's recording process. "There will be a track," Young

Guru said, "and Jay will figure out a flow and a concept for it, if it isn't already in the track. He'll then start pacing around the studio, mumbling to himself. He calls it his 'rain man' thing, and it's a mental exercise where he creates lines and will keep saying them over and over to himself, until he has them memorized. He'll construct a whole verse or pattern in that way. Once he has the verse memorized, he'll go into the booth to recite it."

Jay-Z had told MTV about his recording process two years earlier: "No paper, no pen, just listen to the music."

Jay-Z's unique style definitely worked for him. In October 2000, he released his fifth album in as many years, *The Dynasty: Roc La Familia*. With each previous album, Jay-Z had tried to make things bigger and better: bigger producers, bigger guest stars. But this time, he decided to take a different approach that hopefully would sell records and help expand his record label at the same time.

Instead of superstar contributors, *The Dynasty* was full of up-and-comers who were signed by Roc-A-Fella Records. They were artists the label had hoped to promote and make successful. What better way to accomplish that feat than to pair them up on a record with the biggest, best-selling rapper on the planet?

The Dynasty was a huge risk. Sure, everyone loved Jay-Z, but no one knew who most of the other performers on the record were. But like most everything Jay-Z did at this time, the risk paid off. Mostly because Jay-Z's name was on the cover, *The Dynasty* was the top-selling album in the country the first week it was released. Its singles included the Neptunes-produced "I Just Wanna Love U (Give It 2 Me)," "Change the Game," and "Guilty Until Proven Innocent." The latter song featured a catchy chorus sung by R&B singer R. Kelly. The lyrics centered on the assault charges filed against Jay-Z for the previous year's stabbing incident.

The most notable contributor to benefit from the exposure *The Dynasty* gave him was a young producer-rapper from Chicago, Illinois, named Kanye West, who soon would become a superstar in his own right. On *The Dynasty*, West was responsible for creating the beat behind the song "This Can't Be Life." Other artists who were lesser known at the time but benefited from performing with Jay-Z on *The Dynasty* included Beanie Sigel, Memphis Bleek, Amil, and Pharrell Williams, a member of the Neptunes.

Critics recognized that Jay-Z's latest album was more of a compilation of Roc-A-Fella acts than a typical Jay-Z release. Some even said they believed Jay-Z was a guest star on his own record. That did not mean critics thought the album was terrible. Overall, they gave it mixed reviews. *Village Voice* said, "Jay-Z is in fine form throughout, but the production sounds a bit flat. . . . As usual, Bleek raps like he's on autopilot, boiling down Jay-Z's personality into a charmless caricature. . . . The most alarming thing about *Roc La Familia* is the occasional whiff of desperation. . . . What do you do after you've conquered the world? Like the Wu-Tang Clan, Jay-Z doesn't really have an answer . . . everyone's trying too hard."

Though Jay-Z had somehow managed to avoid too large an entanglement in the prime years of the West Coast–East Coast rap feud, he was unable to avoid the battle for his home turf that occurred after the coastal feud had all but ended in the early 2000s. That new battle was strictly on the East Coast. It was the battle for supremacy there. Jay-Z was New York's top dog, and he was at the center of the battle.

During rap's earliest days, when it was only known as an inner-city street art, "battling" was what the art form was all about. MCs would take turns trying to lyrically one-up each other, until whatever crowd that was watching them declared a winner.

Quick-witted and quick-mouthed Jay-Z frequently won those street battles. But even when rap left the streets, those battles continued. Instead of battling each other live and encircled by listeners, artists began to take shots at each other on records and through the media. The most noteworthy New York City battle took place in the early 2000s between Jay-Z and Nasir "Nas" Jones.

Nas was a Long Island City, New York, rapper who, like Jay-Z, had sold millions of albums during the 1990s. Exactly where the rivalry began is unclear, but the two rappers and their protégés had traded jabs in public and on various recordings over the years. What is clear, however, is that each rapper released at least one signature song that directly attacked the other person. Jay-Z's song was "Takeover," which mentioned Nas by name four times. Jay-Z took Nas to task for his lack of productivity and called him "lame."

Nas' song attacking Jay-Z was called "Ether." It also mentioned Jay-Z by name four times and accused him of selling out and making money on the death of his friend, the Notorious B.I.G. Fans of both rappers took sides. The feud continued for a few years, but eventually Nas and Jay-Z made up. Jay-Z later signed Nas to Def Jam, the record label he was in charge of. The two even performed together onstage.

Nas later said that when he and Jay-Z met in person for the first time after they started fighting, Jay-Z did not say anything about their issues. Instead, he asked Nas if he was doing okay because his mother had recently died. Nas said that meant a lot to him and made him believe Jay-Z was not such a bad guy after all.

In addition to being the song made famous due to its attacks on Nas, the Kanye West-produced "Takeover" also was the second song—and one of the most popular—on Jay-Z's sixth studio album. That album was called *The Blueprint*. Jay-Z decided to release *The Blueprint* a week early to avoid the bootlegging that had hurt sales on his previous release. He avoided that problem but again suffered from bad timing.

The Blueprint was released on September 11, 2001, the same day the deadliest terrorist attacks in American history took place in New York City and Washington, D. C. There is no way to know how big an impact those attacks had on sales of Jay-Z's record. But it still managed to sell more than 400,000 copies in the first week it was available—and it debuted at number one on the Billboard charts.

"At this point in time," wrote *Allmusic*, "nobody in New York could match Jay-Z rhyme for rhyme and nobody in New York had fresher beats." As he had after the school shooting in Colorado, Jay-Z donated a portion of each ticket sold from his subsequent tour to help the victims of the September 11 attacks.

The criminal charges from 1999's stabbing of Un Rivera, which were still pending when *The Blueprint* was recorded, appeared to again have little if any impact on Jay-Z's ability to produce new music and hit songs. It only took him a few weeks to record *The Blueprint*, and he performed nearly all the raps on the album. The exception to that was "Renegade." That song costarred Detroit, Michigan, rap superstar Eminem. It was about Jay-Z's childhood in the ghetto and Eminem's struggles in dealing with success.

Other songs on *The Blueprint* dealt with Jay-Z's love of women ("Girls, Girls, Girls"), living the high life ("Jigga That Nigga"), and about how he overcame the odds to become successful ("Izzo [H.O.V.A.]"). "Hova" was one of the many pseudonyms Jay-Z has had over the years. The word is short for "Jayhova," which is similar to the word *Jehova*. With that nickname, Jay-Z was implying that he was a musical god. In terms of sales, he pretty much was one.

In all, *The Blueprint* was considered the best of Jay-Z's albums since his first one five years earlier. More than ten years after its release, *The Blueprint*— like *Reasonable Doubt*—continued to make critics' lists of the best records of all time.

The Blueprint marked the beginning of the most prolific period of Jay-Z's career. During this period, he found time to perform an intimate concert that was recorded and released as an episode of MTV's popular *Unplugged* series. The show featured Jay-Z alternately seated and standing at the front of the stage, rapping while a small group of vocalists sang, and the Roots played acoustic instruments behind him. It was held at MTV Studios in New York City.

Jay-Z also continued his previous record-a-year pace, releasing *The Blueprint²: The Gift & The Curse* in November 2002. *The Blueprint²* was a double album, filled with twenty-five songs of various styles. Kanye West was back as a featured producer, alongside Just Blaze, Timbaland, the Neptunes, and others. Other big-time musical collaborators were brought on board again too, including Dr. Dre, Lenny Kravitz, and Beyoncé Knowles of the all-female singing group Destiny's Child.

Jay-Z and Beyoncé teamed up on the song "'03 Bonnie & Clyde," trading verses in the song's chorus about how all they really need in life is their girlfriend/ boyfriend. It turns out the two musicians' lines had real-life meaning behind them. Jay-Z and Beyoncé actually were dating when they recorded that song.

Born in Houston, Texas, on September 4, 1981, Beyoncé was twenty-one years old when she and Jay-Z recorded "'03 Bonnie & Clyde." She was not a typical twenty-one-year-old though. She already had won Grammy Awards and sold millions of records, thanks to hit songs she had recorded with Destiny's

Child, including "Jumpin' Jumpin'," "Bills, Bills, Bills," "Say My Name," "Survivor," and "Bootylicious."

Their relationship was a pairing of superstars, but one which they somehow managed to keep out of the public eye. From the start, Jay-Z and Beyoncé vowed to keep their personal relationship private. They would not talk about it in any of the many interviews they conducted. It was their belief that their relationship would benefit by keeping it between themselves. Beyoncé had long held that belief, ever since she once told a member of the media that she did not have a boyfriend, and it became a huge deal.

"They wanted to make me the most desperate thing in the world," she told MTV in 2007. "It was, like, on the cover everywhere: 'Beyoncé is lonely. We need to find her a boyfriend.' So I [decided] I shouldn't even talk about my personal life, because it just makes it a lot easier. And I know people speculate, and I know people wonder, and I respect that and understand that because I've always wondered about people. I mean, before I was a celebrity I did the same thing, so I know people are interested." But she said she soon realized, "I'm a singer, I'll talk about writing songs all you want. But when it comes to certain personal things any normal person wouldn't tell people they don't know, I just feel like I don't have to [talk about it]."

Critics talked a lot about *The Blueprint²: The Gift & The Curse*. Many had issues with it nearly as much as they had loved the first *Blueprint*. One *Entertainment Weekly* reviewer said, "It reminds me of nearly every other double CD. It could have been a good single disc. I give it a C." *Allmusic*'s review was mixed: "It's clear Jay-Z's in control even here, and though his raps can't compete with the concentrated burst on *The Blueprint*, there's at least as many great tracks on tap, if only listeners have enough time to find them."

The general public found those great tracks. And they found them quickly, just as they had every recent Jay-Z album. More than a half-million people bought *The Blueprint²* in its first week, giving Jay-Z another number one album. Still, less than a year later, Jay-Z appeared to have agreed with critics who said the album was too bloated. He took *The Blueprint²* and pared it down to a single CD that he named *Blueprint 2.1*.

Jay-Z then returned the favor to Beyoncé. He offered his rapping and producing talents to her on several songs of her debut solo album, *Dangerously in Love*, which was released in 2003. Jay-Z's name and assistance helped give Beyoncé a certain street credibility she never had before with Destiny's Child. Beyoncé told MTV at the time, "He's helped me a lot on my album. He helped me write some of the songs and . . . actually, before the hip-hop [part] was in ['Crazy in Love'], some people didn't even accept it as much. He gave the song exactly what it needed." "Crazy in Love" became the number one song in the United States and several other countries.

His contributions with Beyoncé were just a few of the collaborations Jay-Z participated in during this time period. He also worked with Mary J. Blige, Eminem, Outkast, R. Kelly, and Aaliyah—with whom he once was linked romantically. Other pre-Beyoncé romantic relationships Jay-Z was rumored to be in included ones with actress Rosario Dawson and rappers Amil and Foxy Brown.

Though it may seem as if Jay-Z was spreading himself a bit thin, he never seemed to lack enough time to create his own music. And he never stopped producing it at a rapid pace. In 2003, exactly a year after his previous record, Jay-Z released *The Black Album*. Public response to the fourteen-song disc, Jay-Z's eighth, was nearly identical to that of his previous releases. Again, it sold nearly a half-million copies in its first week and debuted as the number one album in the country. Critics liked the album much better than the previous one. *The Black Album* opened with a brief interlude followed by an autobiographical song called "December 4th." The song's title also happened to be Jay-Z's birthday.

However, *The Black Album* was different from all the others in one important sense. Prior to its release, Jay-Z had declared that *The Black Album* would be the last one he would ever make. Jay-Z said he was retiring from music. Retirement was something Jay-Z had threatened to do several times before, so not everyone took him seriously. Those who did believe him thought he was leaving while he was still on top. "If the most definitive part of his legacy will be the end, then *The Black Album* gives you Jay-Z at all his stages," *Vibe* magazine wrote. "The masterful lyrical content leaves no question as to how Jay feels he should be remembered."

Jay-Z said he was retiring because his best work was behind him and the competition that once inspired him hardly existed anymore. "The game ain't hot," he told the *New York Times*. "I love when someone makes a hot album and then you've got to make a hot album. I love that. But it ain't hot. . . . I don't ever want to get to the point where I'm just making music because I know how to make a hit record. I want to make it because I love to make it. For me to do that I need to feed off other things." Those other things always had been other MCs. In Jay-Z's opinion, he had left his competition in the dust. There was no one left for him to compete with anymore.

Was he ever going to make another record? *AllHipHop.com* asked him that same question. Jay-Z's answer: "If you ask me today, of course I would say no. I'm a human being so I try to give myself a little window, but in a few years, if I'm withdrawn somewhere [I might change my mind]. I don't want to box myself in a corner." Jay-Z definitely was going out while he was on top of his game. *The Black Album* was a hit, selling millions of copies.

During his retirement period, Jay-Z was asked by *blackfilm.com* what advice he would give to children who wanted to get into the rap business. Jay-Z said he would tell them, "Don't. . . . That would weed out all the people that aren't that serious about it. If it's truly your passion and something that you really love, there will be a lot of doors slammed in your face and you have to keep going. You just need that belief in yourself that it's going to happen for you and you need it wholeheartedly. . . . Doors will be slammed. I could have said that this wasn't for me and do something else, but I looked right in the face of the corporation, and told them that they're wrong."

Chapter 5

RETIRED, MARRIED, AND DECODED

I t was soon revealed that Jay-Z's definition of retirement was not exactly the same as most people's. He did not take a permanent vacation to a sunny area near a warm ocean. He did not spend his days watching television, playing golf, or playing card games.

When Jay-Z, now thirty-four years old, said he was retiring, he actually meant that he was retiring from certain activities. He no longer planned to tour, and he no longer planned to make his own records. He did stop doing both those things—temporarily, at least—but he also spent the extra time he now had working harder than ever at other endeavors that he previously only had time to dabble in.

He spent more time collaborating with others, including rock band Linkin Park. The artists even released a short album titled *Collision Course,* which featured mashups of Linkin Park and Jay-Z songs. He released a film of his life and his Madison Square Garden retirement concert, called *Fade to Black.* He accepted a job as president of Def Jam Records. He spent more time developing and expanding the 40/40 Club—a Manhattan sports bar, lounge, and restaurant he owned—and his Rocawear clothing company. In 2004, the first year of Jay-Z's retirement, Rocawear did $300 million in business.

In addition, Jay-Z signed a multimillion-dollar endorsement deal with athletic shoemaker Reebok. He was the first non-athlete to sign such a deal with the company, which released a line of shoes named after him called S. Carter. The shoes were the fastest-selling shoes in the history of the company.

Jay-Z also bought a small stake in the New Jersey Nets basketball team. Later, he helped the team relocate to a new arena in his hometown of Brooklyn. He even founded a film company. Clearly, Jay-Z was not retired.

To most people, Jay-Z appeared to be living a charmed life. He had tons of money and was donating large amounts of it to various charities. He had a beautiful and talented girlfriend. But Jay-Z still had his share of hang-ups, some of which stemmed from the abandonment he had faced in his childhood.

One day, Jay-Z approached his mother and told her he felt he would never be happy in a relationship. Gloria Carter took action. She knew what her son needed to fix his problem. She set up a reunion between Jay-Z and his father, whom she had kept in touch with over the years. Jay-Z had not seen his father in twenty years.

"My mother saw some of the comments I'd made about him on records as me still holding on to pain from my childhood," Jay-Z told *Vibe* magazine in 2004. "She was really working both ends, because my father hadn't gone to her to set up a meeting; he was too proud. He didn't want me to think that he was trying to get at me because I was this millionaire or famous rapper." Jay-Z finally agreed to a reunion.

On the day the reunion was supposed to occur, Jay-Z sent a car to pick up his father. But his father was not there. Jay-Z said that was enough. He had reached out and his dad had not showed up. Now Jay-Z was done with the man. His mother told him to give his dad another chance. He said yes, and she set up another reunion. "She knew how alcoholism had eaten away most of his organs and how little time he was actually working with. So she pushed again," Jay-Z said. His father—who it turned out was living just a few minutes away from his son his whole life—showed up the second time.

When Jay-Z finally laid eyes on his father, he could not believe what he was seeing. He said looking at his father was like looking in the mirror. Both men were tall. Both were slim.

"I'd pretty much built up a wall to that emotion [for his father], which wasn't healthy," Jay-Z told radio host Howard Stern in 2010. "I went in to [the reunion] with a lot of anger, thinking I was gonna tell him off, and it didn't happen like that."

When Jay-Z met with his father, the older man had been ill for a long time. He died a short time later.

Jay-Z told Stern he had forgiven his father for leaving him and finally realized how deeply the abandonment had affected him his whole life: "Your father, growing up, is like Superman to you. He's everything, so once you feel that sort of hurt, you never allow yourself to get close to that feeling. You don't even wanna feel that good because you know the flip-side of that. You don't let people get that close so they won't hurt you."

During his retirement, Jay-Z also had to deal with a lawsuit from his former friend, R. Kelly. Kelly sued Jay-Z for $75 million for damages he claimed he received after Jay-Z kicked him off their co-headlining Best of Both Worlds tour in 2004. Kelly said that during the tour, Jay-Z purposely made sure the lighting was not good when Kelly was onstage. He also said that Jay-Z threatened violence against him. The suit was settled out of court for an undisclosed amount of money.

In November 2006, Jay-Z's work-filled "retirement" ended, less than three years after it had begun. The "unretirement" he had declared during a concert in 2005 was made official by the release of a new Jay-Z album, his ninth, called *Kingdom Come.*

From the start, it was clear the general public still had an interest in Jay-Z's music. In fact, *Kingdom Come* sold more than 600,000 copies during the first week it was released. That was more than any previous Jay-Z record had sold. Music critics, on the other hand, were not as easily impressed with the comeback kid. *Uncut* magazine rated *Kingdom Come* only three stars out of ten, saying "The premise behind *Kingdom Come*, fairly predictably, is that he has been forced to cut short his retirement because hip hop needs him back. Whilst a gift for converting arrogance into entertainment has always been one of Jay-Z's strongest suits, *Kingdom Come* skirts perilously close to the showboating that marred 2002's bloated double album, *The Blueprint 2.*"

Time magazine believed, "The album's Who's Who of producers, including Dr. Dre and Kanye West, normally could be relied on to spice up the duller patches, but the riffs either sound recycled or, more disturbingly, like Herb Alpert-era smooth jazz. (Not a positive trend for this or any other genre.) Jay-Z may yet have more to say, but he doesn't say it here."

Kingdom Come was a major departure from Jay-Z's earlier records. Featuring vocal contributions from Usher, Beyoncé, John Legend, and Chris Martin of Coldplay, the record was more mature sounding than any of his earlier work. The record's creator mostly agreed. He told CNN that he felt he needed to change his music a little bit, to make it different, if he wanted continued success. "The responsibility is to keep pushing forward," he told CNN, "to not rely on the old gimmicks and old tricks. . . . In the beginning [rap] was all shock. Now it has a responsibility to push it forward, to tell deeper stories with deeper meaning. And to entertain."

Kingdom Come's subject matter was not simply relegated to the hip-hop world, as it had been in much of Jay-Z's previous records. In the song "Minority Report," for example, Jay-Z tackled the politics behind the then-recent Hurricane Katrina, which killed nearly two thousand people in the southern United States. He rapped about how the poor people were being overlooked and how the U. S. government was not supplying aid quickly enough to those stranded on the rooftops of buildings surrounded by water. He even talked about how he donated money to the cause. But because he did not volunteer his time, he felt as if he had overlooked the victims too.

In his book *Decoded*, Jay-Z explained his motive for writing the song. He wrote, "I wanted to do a song about Katrina, but I also wanted the song to be about how what we saw during the hurricane was just an extreme example of the [stuff] that was already happening in New Orleans. The young guys there were motivated by the same desperation as the guy who loots the store after the hurricane for diapers and formula. Both are just trying to survive in a storm."

Jay-Z regained his street cred less than a year later with the release of *American Gangster*. The album was a concept album, meaning that all fifteen songs were based on a common theme. *American Gangster*'s theme was inspired by the movie of the same name starring Denzel Washington and Russell Crowe. The movie was about the life of Frank Lucas, a major drug dealer in New York during the 1960s and 1970s. Washington played Lucas in the film. *Rolling Stone* described Jay-Z's reason for creating the album: "Seeing parallels between the life of gangster Frank Lucas and his own early days, Jay-Z used the film's narrative as a template to tell his own story in stark, vivid language, set against a backdrop of gritty soul hooks."

Aside from a few pop-music moments, the album was rough. It sounded a lot like what most people considered Jay-Z's finest moment, that being his first album, *Reasonable Doubt*. As such, it was not a groundbreaking release, but one that still sold well and received favorable reviews. *American Gangster* was another number one album that eventually sold millions of copies. *The Village Voice* said, "Much like the film (which clocks in at almost three hours), this *Gangster* could've used some trimming. But as last year's poorly received *Kingdom Come* still proved, Jay's misstep is another rapper's highlight. This one's not too shabby either. Even with its shortcomings and some obvious ploys, Jay sets a scene the film couldn't."

Jay-Z quit his job as president of Def Jam Records in 2007, that same year *American Gangster* was released. He eventually signed a $150 million deal with Live Nation, a concert-promotion company that previously had signed other superstar musicians, such as Madonna and U2. The deal gave Live Nation control of Jay-Z's recordings, merchandise, concert tickets, and certain licensing rights to use his name.

The rapper-turned-entrepreneur actually did not release an album of new material in 2008. That did not mean Jay-Z's year was uneventful. In fact, it still was packed with activity, both personal and professional. His biggest personal news of 2008 happened on April 4. That was the day Jay-Z, now thirty-eight years old, quietly married his longtime girlfriend, twenty-six-year-old Beyoncé, in a small ceremony in Jay-Z's penthouse apartment in New York City.

Typically, celebrity weddings—especially when the celebrities are as huge as Jay-Z and Beyoncé—are paparazzi-filled events. Helicopters fly overhead during the ceremony in hopes of catching a photo or some video of the bride, groom, and the rest of the wedding party. There was some of that with this wedding as well, since it was held on a rooftop. But Jay-Z and Beyoncé were able to keep the details of their wedding secret from all but forty or so of their closest friends and family who actually attended the wedding.

As the wedding was taking place, various media outlets found out about it and posted frequent updates on their Web sites. They described which guests had been spotted outside the apartment and what they were wearing (Beyoncé's close friends were wearing white dresses). They described the amount and types of flowers being delivered (50,000–60,000 white orchid blooms). They even mentioned the hiring of the limousine drivers. Even so, few big details of the event found their way out to the general public. The wedding was so secret that all guests were required to leave their cellphones outside before they came in.

Even after they were married, Jay-Z and Beyoncé were quiet about the details of the wedding. Sometimes, they would not even confirm that the wedding actually had happened. When Jay-Z was congratulated in public three days after the wedding, according to *People* magazine, he laughed and said, "I don't know what you're talking about." The magazine also reported that Beyoncé was spotted in public wearing a "huge rock" on her finger on April 8. But it was clear the couple was not going to allow their personal lives to be on public display.

Chapter 6

POLITICS AND MUSIC

During the 2008 presidential election, Jay-Z threw his support behind Barack Obama, a Democratic U. S. senator from Illinois. Obama was vying to become the first African-American president. Jay-Z told Oprah Winfrey, "Before he announced he was running, I met him and we had dinner. I was like, 'Man, this guy is special.' Certain people just glow." Jay-Z spoke favorably of Obama throughout his 2008 campaign and headlined several political rallies in support of the candidate. Obama also played some of the rapper's songs during various campaign stops that year.

After Obama won the presidency, Jay-Z attended his inauguration and noticed how the president-elect was able to bring people of all races together in the name of hope. In 2009, Jay-Z told Winfrey: "The election of Barack Obama sent a strong message. Afterward I said, 'The day that Barack Obama became president, the gangsta became less relevant.' I meant that in a positive way. I meant that we grew up without accountants and lawyers as role models, but now we see something different. There's something else for us to aspire to." Jay-Z also performed a new song at Obama's presidential ball called "History."

As a child, Jay-Z said he and other African Americans around him never much cared who the president was. But he believed things were different now that Obama was president. He told *blackfilm. com*: "Growing up, we never thought voting was important in our neighborhood because no matter who was in office, it didn't affect change where we live. It didn't trickle down to where we live. . . . [Now] we have a choice to vote because of the people that planted that seed fifty years before and they knew they wouldn't see it in their lifetime. They knew the future generations would see it. We have to think like that. We have to affect change now so that forty years from now we will reap the benefits from that."

He later added in an interview with CNN: "It gives us another face, the hope of, 'OK, maybe I can be president of the United States.' It takes someone to do it for you to believe that you can achieve such lofty goals."

Jay-Z's support of Obama was not the first time he had been politically active on a large scale. Two years earlier, Jay-Z had met with the secretary-general of the United Nations, Kofi Annan, and the president of MTV to talk about ways they could help the one billion people in the world who do not have access to safe drinking water. The outcome of the meeting was an MTV special show called *Diary of Jay-Z: Water for Life*.

The program showed Jay-Z traveling to Africa to shine a light on the problem. The goal was to educate young people watching the program about such important global issues that they may not even be aware of.

"I wanted to go to these [countries I've never visited before] to just tour and play music," Jay-Z said. "[However] when you start getting down to Africa and places like that, you see that billions of people don't have access to water. . . . If you bring awareness to other young people, they're gonna see [that] and want to be involved. I'm not a politician—I'm just a regular person with a heart. If you see a problem like that and do nothing about it, there's something wrong with you."

Professionally, Jay-Z's 2008 included a headlining show at England's popular Glastonbury Festival. His selection was a controversial one for the event, which typically featured guitar-driven rock-and-roll bands. The leader of one such band, in fact, spoke out publically against the festival's choice of headliner as soon as the news was made public. "If you break it, people ain't gonna go," Noel Gallagher of the rock band Oasis told the BBC network of the festival. "I'm sorry, but Jay-Z? . . . No chance. I'm not having hip-hop at Glastonbury. It's wrong."

Initially, it looked like Gallagher was right. Ticket sales to the annual event were slow. But when Jay-Z took to the stage—with a popular Oasis song playing as a joke and huge cheers coming from the crowd—the Brooklyn-born rapper proved he belonged. "All that doom and gloom about ticket sales," the event's organizer told Reuters, "but we were completely sold out by Thursday and we had such a younger audience. That was a real triumph to bring hip-hop from the streets of New York to Glastonbury." In 2010, Jay-Z headlined the first day of a similar festival in California called Coachella.

Jay-Z shifted his focus back toward creating his music in 2009. That year, he released *The Blueprint 3*.

When *The Blueprint 3* debuted at number one upon its release in September, it helped Jay-Z set a record. He passed legendary signer Elvis Presley as the all-time leader on the list of number one records by solo artists. It was Jay-Z's eleventh chart-topper. Only the Beatles now had released more best-selling albums than Jay-Z had.

The Blueprint 3 had not been successful based on Jay-Z's popularity alone. It was true that, at this point, the millionaire business mogul could release most anything and it would sell well. His name was such a big deal. But *The Blueprint 3* actually contained some solid work. A few of its songs—including "Run This Town," "D.O.A. (Death of Auto-Tune)," and "Young Forever"—all found their way onto the Billboard charts. One single, "Empire State of Mind," made it all the way to number one. The song featured Alicia Keys singing a "New York"-filled chorus that was at once catchy, inspirational, and powerful.

The pair performed the song together at various locations, including in Yankee Stadium during Game 2 of the 2009 World Series. During the performance, TV cameras showed players from both the home team and the visiting team from Philadelphia bobbing their heads to the beat. The crowd was doing the same and gave Jay-Z and Alicia Keys—both native New Yorkers—a standing ovation when they were done.

Alicia Keys liked the song so much that she recorded and released her own version of it. The song became an anthem for the state of New York. Jay-Z again performed it during the parade honoring the New York Yankees after they won the World Series.

"Empire State of Mind" was a smash with fans and critics alike. The album it was on received mixed reviews from both. *Pitchfork* magazine did not like it, saying it was "the kind of stuck-on-stupid, event-driven money pit that proves while Jay-Z's at a point where he's got no one to answer to but himself, he's still capable of an entire hour of failing to take his own advice." *Entertainment Weekly*, on the other hand, gave *Blueprint 3* a B+ rating, saying, "Even if it lacks the raw power of his earlier work, the album succeeds at its larger goal—reaching maximum commercial blast radius while maintaining its street bona fides. . . . *Blueprint* is hip-hop as big business, and Jay retains his CEO throne."

In 2009, Jay-Z expanded his throne to New York's theater-heavy Broadway street too. He signed on as a producer of a new play called *Fela!* The play was about the life of legendary African musician Fela Anikulapo Kuti. Jay-Z told MTV, "It's an inspiration, about the power of music. Here's a guy that's on the other side of the world who was influenced by James

Brown, who takes this thing and makes his own sort of genre of music. I just think it's fascinating."

It was fascinating enough to Jay-Z that he rearranged his schedule so he could attend the play's opening night. Rearranging an average person's schedule typically is no big deal. But rearranging the schedule of a superstar like Jay-Z can be expensive. In 2009 alone, it is estimated that Jay-Z earned $63 million. Broken down, that is more than $172,000 a day.

Just when it seemed as though there was nothing Jay-Z could do that he had not done before, he found something. He had never written a book. In the mid-2000s, he had worked with an author to write his autobiography. However, he decided after it was finished that he did not want to release it to the public. When he made the decision, he told *Rolling Stone*, "It's too much. For the book, I was interviewed, people close to me were interviewed, so I was learning a lot of things I didn't know as a child. It's not anything I haven't said in the past, in songs. It's just more detailed. . . . You can say exactly how everything went."

The collaborator of that autobiography eventually did work on a book with Jay-Z. Her name was Dream Hampton. In 2010, *Decoded*, the book she cowrote with Jay-Z, was released shortly before Christmas.

The book immediately became a *New York Times* best-seller. It was nowhere near as revealing as the shelved autobiography likely would have been. But *Decoded* was part memoir and part Jay-Z explaining the meaning and reasoning behind the lyrics to some of his best-known songs and some unreleased ones too. The book's format was an unusual one. Instead of a straight biography of Jay-Z's life, it was a collection of essays and lyrics. In the book's epilogue, Jay-Z explained why he wrote it: "People give words power, so banning a word is futile, really. 'Nigga' becomes 'porch monkey' becomes 'coon' and so on if that what's in a person's heart. The key is to change the person. We can change people through conversation, not through censorship. That's why I want people to understand what the words we use—and the stories we tell—are really about. And that's why I wrote this book."

Decoded generally was well received, but some controversy concerning the book did surface. In 2012, a man by the name of Patrick White sued Jay-Z, Hampton, and Random House, the book's publisher. White claimed his computer had been stolen the year before the book came out, and that some of his "expressions/colors/phrases" were taken from that computer and used in *Decoded*. By 2013, that lawsuit had not been settled.

Jay-Z's popularity was near its peak in 2010. Concerts he performed with other stars—including Eminem and U2—sold out in minutes. A collaboration he began recording that year with Kanye West called *Watch the Throne* became another number one hit when it was released the following year. *Allmusic* called the experimental album, "An audacious spectacle of vacuous pomposity as well as one of tremendous lyrical depth."

In a nutshell, that is what it was. The most-celebrated cut off the disc was "Otis," which won a Grammy Award for Best Rap Performance in 2012. The song contained a sample of music by Otis Redding, a popular African-American singer-songwriter most famous for his 1967 song "(Sittin' On) The Dock of the Bay." As was the case with much of Jay-Z's music, and hip-hop music in general, there were samples from many other artists on *Watch the Throne*. Those samples included several from soul legend James Brown.

West and Jay-Z went on a tour of North America in support of the album. The over-the-top tour featured a large set list and was a hit in every city it stopped in. The tour kicked off in Atlanta, Georgia, in October 2011.

USA Today said of the show: "Many in the high-energy crowd remained standing—and swaying and dancing and singing—for the entire 2½-hour show. At one point, as Jay-Z and West performed 'N---as in Paris' from their hit *Watch the Throne* CD, West exhorted the audience to 'Bounce! Bounce!' The resulting stomping had Philips Arena rocking and shaking in a way that it hasn't for the Hawks [Atlanta's professional basketball team] in a long time."

Chapter 7

BEING THERE

In 2011, an in-depth biography of Jay-Z's life was finally released in book form. But it was not the one Jay-Z had worked on years earlier with author Dream Hampton. It was not another edition of *Decoded* either. The new book, called *Empire State of Mind: How Jay-Z Went From Street Corner to Corner Office*, was an unauthorized biography written by Zack O'Malley Greenburg, a writer for *Forbes* magazine. The book's promotional material read: "You can wake up to the local radio station playing Jay-Z's latest hit, spritz yourself with his 9IX cologne, slip on a pair of his Rocawear jeans, lace up your Reebok S. Carter sneakers, catch a Nets basketball game in the afternoon, and grab dinner at The Spotted Pig [a New York restaurant co-owned by Jay-Z] before heading to an evening performance of the Jay-Z-backed Broadway musical *Fela!* and a nightcap at his 40/40 Club. He'll profit at every turn of your day."

Greenburg spent more than a year interviewing people who had known Jay-Z after he had become famous and uncovered some never-before-reported details about Jay-Z's failed business dealings. Dealings, Greenburg believed, Jay-Z wanted kept secret. One of those dealings included a partnership with carmaker Chrysler to produce a limited edition Jay-Z Jeep. According to the book, the Jeep would have been blue with twenty-two-inch wheels, leather seats, and a sound system that came equipped with every Jay-Z song. But the deal fell through, and the Jeep never happened.

Greenburg's book also delved into Jay-Z's childhood through stories of those who knew him well, including high school classmates and childhood friends: "[T]he young Jay-Z indeed became troublingly detached. The worst manifestation of this occurred . . . when Jay-Z shot his drugged-out older brother in the shoulder for stealing a ring." Jaz-O, Jay-Z's mentor and former partner, told Greenburg, "His brother didn't press charges partly because his brother knew he was wrong . . . he felt to an extent that it was an accident. He understood that it was his little brother who couldn't beat his big brother and was just trying to intimidate him."

Greenburg said he had tried to interview Jay-Z for the book but was denied access to the superstar. After writing the book, on numerous occasions, Greenburg said he tried to ask Jay-Z what he thought of it. One day in 2012, he got his opportunity. Greenburg introduced himself to Jay-Z and told him who he was. Greenburg wrote in *Forbes* that Jay-Z replied: "That book was horrible!"

Any negative public relations Jay-Z may have experienced from the release of Greenburg's book were easily overshadowed by one of the biggest developments in his life. Shortly after the book was released, on January 7, 2012, Jay-Z and Beyoncé's first child was born at Lennox Hill Hospital in New York City. They paid $1.3 million to rent out an entire floor of the hospital and hired extra security guards so they could have their privacy.

The couple—thirty-year-old Beyoncé and forty-two-year-old Jay-Z—had a daughter. She was named Blue Ivy Carter. The new parents soon released a statement about her birth: "Hello Hello Baby Blue! We are happy to announce the arrival of our beautiful daughter, Blue Ivy Carter, born on Saturday, January 7, 2012. Her birth was emotional and extremely peaceful, we are in heaven. She was delivered naturally at a healthy 7 lbs. and it was the best experience of both of our lives. We are thankful to everyone for all your prayers, well wishes, love and support. —Beyoncé & JAY Z."

The name Blue Ivy certainly was unique, but the color blue had played a role in many of Jay-Z's creations, most recently in the title of each of the three *Blueprint* records.

Many of the couple's emotions likely were tied to the difficulties Beyoncé had in getting pregnant in the first place, and the miscarriage she had before Blue Ivy's birth. Like most of the couple's private life, the miscarriage was not known to the general public. That is until two days after Blue Ivy's birth, when Jay-Z released a song called "Glory." In it, he rapped about Beyoncé's previous miscarriage, how happy he was to have a daughter, and what he hopes and expects the future will hold for her.

At the end of the song, you can hear Blue Ivy crying. The song soon cracked the Billboard charts. Because Blue Ivy Carter's name [written as B.I.C.] was listed in the song's credits, she became the youngest person ever to appear on a Billboard chart.

As might be expected with two superstar parents, Blue Ivy also became the most popular baby in the world. Everyone wanted to see photos of her. Her parents have managed to mostly shield her from the public's eye, but they also have thought ahead to the future. Shortly after their daughter's birth, Jay-Z and Beyoncé filed an application to trademark the name Blue Ivy. Some believe plans are in the works to release a line of baby products under that name.

Whatever happens to Blue Ivy, one thing is a near certainty. She will not grow up in poverty like her father did. There will be no street hustling, no shooting her siblings, and no being shot at.

As of 2013, her mother's net worth was estimated at $300 million. Her father's net worth was somewhere in the $475 million range. Together, the two performers were worth nearly $1 billion. So not only are they one of the most recognizable celebrity couples in the world, but they are one of the richest too. They can afford to buy each other expensive gifts—such as the $5 million white gold-and-diamond watch Beyoncé bought Jay-Z on his forty-third birthday. And they can afford to take care of their daughter. Jay-Z has said that always will be his number one priority.

Throughout his life, Jay-Z often talked about how he wanted to be a father someday. He has sworn over and over again that he would be a better father than he felt his dad was and that he would never leave his child behind.

"Providing—that's not love," he told *GQ* magazine in 2011. *"Being there*—that's more important." In fact, Jay-Z's first goal in life is to make sure Blue Ivy, and any other children he and Beyoncé may have, are taken care of. "As far as who we are and where we come from," he told CNN, "we haven't acquired wealth to hand down and give the opportunity to the next generation. So my goal is that my next generation can have a better start than I had. It won't have to start so far [down]. We have to give opportunity."

And will he let Blue Ivy listen to his R-rated records? Of course, he told *GQ*. When the time is right.

Trying to determine which direction Jay-Z will focus his attention on next is nearly impossible. Rocawear has expanded its offerings to include purses, cologne, sunglasses, and more. The products are available in stores across the United States. Although Jay-Z sold the rights to the brand in 2007 to Iconix Brand Group, he still maintains creative control of it and a stake in the company. He sold the company because it made good sense for him as a businessman.

Rocawear is estimated to sell hundreds of millions of dollars of its products each year. Jay-Z's other non-music business ventures are numerous and profitable.

His 40/40 Club sports bars can now be found in three East Coast locations.

Jay-Z is also still a big player in the sports world. His entertainment company, Roc Nation, is getting into the sports agency business. The new company will be called Roc Nation Sports. Jay-Z's firm has already signed its first big-name client: New York Yankees superstar Robinson Cano. Jay-Z still needs to sell his stake in the Brooklyn Nets so that he himself can sign NBA players to his new sports agency.

Jay-Z has also dabbled in real estate. And he still contributes to those who need help. His Shawn Carter Scholarship Foundation has given more than $1.3 million to help more than 750 needy students pay for college.

Jay-Z has even taken a recent political stance that once would have earned him ridicule among his fellow rappers. After President Barack Obama came out in support of gay marriage in May 2012, his longtime supporter Jay-Z was asked his opinion on the issue. He told CNN, "What people do in their own homes is their business and you can choose to love whoever you love. That's their business. [It] is no different than discriminating against blacks. It's discrimination, plain and simple."

Rap used to be a mostly homophobic art form. Jay-Z's stance could help change that.

Musically, Jay-Z continues to work with other artists and perform select live shows. In the summer of 2013, he and pop star Justin Timberlake embarked on a tour of several major U. S. cities. Less than a year earlier, in September 2012, he performed eight shows in a row in the new Barclays Center in Brooklyn, New York. Every one of the shows—which were the first-ever events staged in the arena—sold out. During the first of those shows, Jay-Z told the crowd: "I've been on many stages all around the world. Nothing feels like this, Brooklyn!"

For Jay-Z, who many polls have ranked as the greatest MC of all time, it was good to be home. He has sold some 50 million records, and in many ways is a much different person from what he had been when he was growing up down the street. But in many ways he is also still the same.

"People look at you weird saying, 'You changed.' Like you worked that hard to stay the same," he said.

> You're doing all this for a reason. And what happens most of the time is that people change. People change around you because they start treating you different because of your success. So you are changing. You don't change the core of who you are. The things you believe, the things you love, and the things you die for. And your principles. You don't change that. . . . You

can't do the same things. You can't hang on the corner. [And] no matter how far you are you still have that stigma on you of where you come from when you walk inside the door.

CHRONOLOGY

1969—Shawn Corey Carter is born December 4 in Brooklyn, New York.

1980—Father Adnis Reeves abandons family.

1982—Shoots older brother in the shoulder for stealing his jewelry.

Mid-1980s—Attends high school with Notorious B.I.G. and Busta Rhymes.

1989—Appears on Jaz-O's "Hawaiian Sophie" single.

1995—Creates independent record label, Roc-A-Fella Records, with Damon Dash and Kareem Biggs.

1996—Releases debut album, *Reasonable Doubt*.

1997—Releases second album, *In My Lifetime, Vol. 1*.

1998—Releases third album, *Volume 2 . . . Hard Knock Life*; song "Hard Knock Life (Ghetto Anthem)" becomes big hit.

1999—Creates Rocawear clothing line; releases fourth album, *Vol. 3 . . . Life and Times of S. Carter*; accused of stabbing record executive Lance "Un" Rivera in New York.

2000—Releases fifth album, *The Dynasty: Roc La Familia.*

2001—Begins feud with Nas; references him in "Takeover" and Nas responds with "Ether"; releases sixth album, *The Blueprint.*

2002—Releases seventh album, *The Blueprint²: The Gift & The Curse*; two singles, "Excuse Me Miss" and "'03 Bonnie & Clyde" featuring future wife Beyoncé Knowles.

2003—Releases eighth album, *The Black Album*; opens first 40/40 Club in New York City; collaborates with R. Kelly and releases album *The Best of Both Worlds*; holds retirement concert at Madison Square Garden that will later be featured in the movie *Fade to Black.*

2004—Releases second collaborative album with R. Kelly, *Unfinished Business*; collaborates with Linkin Park; wins Best Rap/Sung Collaboration Grammy for "Numb/Encore"; named president of Def Jam Records and takes control of both that and Roc-A-Fella Records after Dash and Biggs sell their interests; begins dating Beyoncé Knowles.

2005—Becomes an investor in Carol's Daughter, a line of beauty products; opens second 40/40 Club in Atlantic City, New Jersey.

2006—Releases comeback album, *Kingdom Come*; song "Show Me What You Got" from *Kingdom Come* is leaked a month early and FBI investigates; meets the United Nations secretary-general and pledges to raise awareness on the global water shortage during his upcoming world tour; produces a documentary entitled *Diary of Jay-Z: Water for Life.*

2007—Sells the rights to Rocawear for $204 million but retains his stake in the company; releases tenth album, *American Gangster*; opens third 40/40 Club location in the Venetian Hotel in Las Vegas, Nevada.

2008—Vacates his position as president of Def Jam Records; headlines 2008 Glastonbury Festival in England, the first major hip-hop artist to do so; headlines other summer festivals; marries Beyoncé Knowles; becomes active in the presidential election, supporting Barack Obama and helping send people to voting polls.

2009—Parts ways with Def Jam Records and signs with Live Nation Entertainment; starts his Twitter page; releases *The Blueprint 3* three days early because of anticipation from fans; *The Blueprint 3* is eleventh No.1 hit on the Billboard 200, beating Elvis Presley's record.

2010—Releases song "Stranded (Haiti Mon Amour)"
with Rihanna, Bono, and the Edge; performs
shows with Eminem; publishes memoir, *Decoded*;
collaborates with Kanye West on *Watch the
Throne*.

2011—Launches a lifestyle blog-format Web site.

2012—Daughter, Blue Ivy Carter, born January 7.

SELECTED DISCOGRAPHY

1996—*Reasonable Doubt*

1997—*In My Lifetime, Vol. 1*

1998—*Vol. 2 ... Hard Knock Life*

1999—*Vol. 3 ... Life and Times of S. Carter*

2000—*The Dynasty: Roc La Familia*

2001—*The Blueprint*

2001—*Unplugged*

2002—*The Blueprint^2: The Gift & The Curse*

2003—*The Black Album*

2004—*Unfinished Business* (with R. Kelly)

2006—*Kingdom Come*

2007—*American Gangster*

2009—*The Blueprint 3*

2011—*Watch the Throne* (with Kanye West)

2012—*Live in Brooklyn*

GLOSSARY

bootlegging—Selling something, such as music, illegally.

collaboration—A project someone does with another person or persons.

cred—Short for "credibility."

critic—Someone who works for a newspaper, magazine, or other media outlet who evaluates the works of others.

endorsement—An agreement to represent something, such as a product.

epilogue—The conclusion of a book or speech.

gangsta—Slang for "gangster"; a form of rap music.

ghetto—An extremely poor portion of a city, often inhabited by those belonging to one or more minority groups.

headlining—Working as the star of a show.

homophobic—Reflecting fear and often hatred of homosexuals.

hustler—A person who makes money through illegal means, such as selling drugs.

inauguration—Formal ceremony that officially places a person in office.

interlude—A short piece of music or performance placed between two longer pieces.

ironic—Coincidental or odd.

MC—Short for "emcee"; master of ceremonies.

misogynistic—Reflecting a hatred of women.

principles—Accepted standards of behavior.

projects—Short for "housing projects"; a publicly owned and operated housing development, typically filled with lower-income residents.

prolific—Highly productive.

protégé—A person who learns a trade or craft, such as music, from someone else.

rap—To talk or sing to the beat of music.

record—Short for "recording"; a piece of music.

superfluity—Excess.

theme—The subject of a work of art.

underground music—Music that exists outside mainstream society or culture.

FURTHER READING

Abrams, Dennis. *Jay-Z.* New York: Chelsea House, 2008.

Hillstrom, Laurie Collier. *Jay-Z.* Detroit: Lucent Books, 2010.

Hoblin, Paul. *Jay-Z: Hip-Hop Mogul.* Minneapolis, Minn.: ABDO Publishing Company, 2012.

Spilsbury, Richard. *Jay-Z.* Chicago: Heinemann Library, 2013.

INTERNET ADDRESSES

Forbes.com: Jay-Z
<http://www.forbes.com/profile/jay-z/>

Biography.com: Jay-Z
<http://www.biography.com/people/jay-z-507696>

INDEX